AGATHA CHRISTIE

MURDER ON THE ORIENT EXPRESS

ADAPTED BY FRANÇOIS RIVIÈRE
ILLUSTRATED BY SOLIDOR

HARPER

HARPER

An imprint of HarperCollins*Publishers*
77-85 Fulham Palace Road
Hammersmith, London W6 8JB
www.harpercollins.co.uk

First published by HARPER 2007
1

Comic book edition published in France as *Le Crime de l'Orient-Express*
© EP Editions 2003
Based on *Murder on the Orient Express* © 1933 by Agatha Christie Limited,
a Chorion Company. All rights reserved.
www.agathachristie.com

Adapted by François Rivière. Illustrated by Solidor. Colour by Cécile Vergult.
English edition edited by David Brawn.

ISBN-13 978-0-00-724658-8
ISBN-10 0-00-724658-7

Printed and bound in Singapore by Imago

ISTANBUL, WINTER 1932...

Monsieur Poirot?

?!

Ah, Monsieur Bouc! You have my ticket?

It is extraordinary, Monsieur Poirot. All the world elects to travel tonight! There are no more first-class sleeping berths left!

Do not distress yourself, *mon ami.* I will travel in an ordinary carriage.

Pierre! Please put Monsieur Poirot in berth number 7.

Merci, Monsieur Bouc. I must get aboard. See you later!

There must be a mistake!

Sorry, Mr MacQueen, but the train is full. You must share this cabin tonight with Monsieur Poirot.

1

THE ORIENT EXPRESS STARTS ITS THREE-DAY JOURNEY ACROSS EUROPE ...

Nnnnnnn!

Ah, Monsieur Poirot! You slept well, I trust?

Very well, mon ami ...

Look! That ugly old lady is the Russian Princess Dragomiroff. She is extremely rich!

I'm famished!

And that is Samuel Ratchett, the respectable American. Mr MacQueen's boss.

Mrs Hubbard is also American. It is unusual to see such an, *er*, cosmopolitan group on the Orient Express!

No doubt, *cher ami*. No doubt ...

Well, well. I thought Colonel Arbuthnot and Mary Debenham knew each other, yet they sit apart ...

Mary... if you only knew how I want to see you out of all this!

Hush! When it's all over, when it's behind us. Then ...

Come, Mary!

How very strange ...

Oh! I'm...sorry!

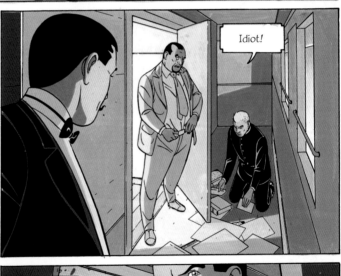

Idiot!

How rude!

3

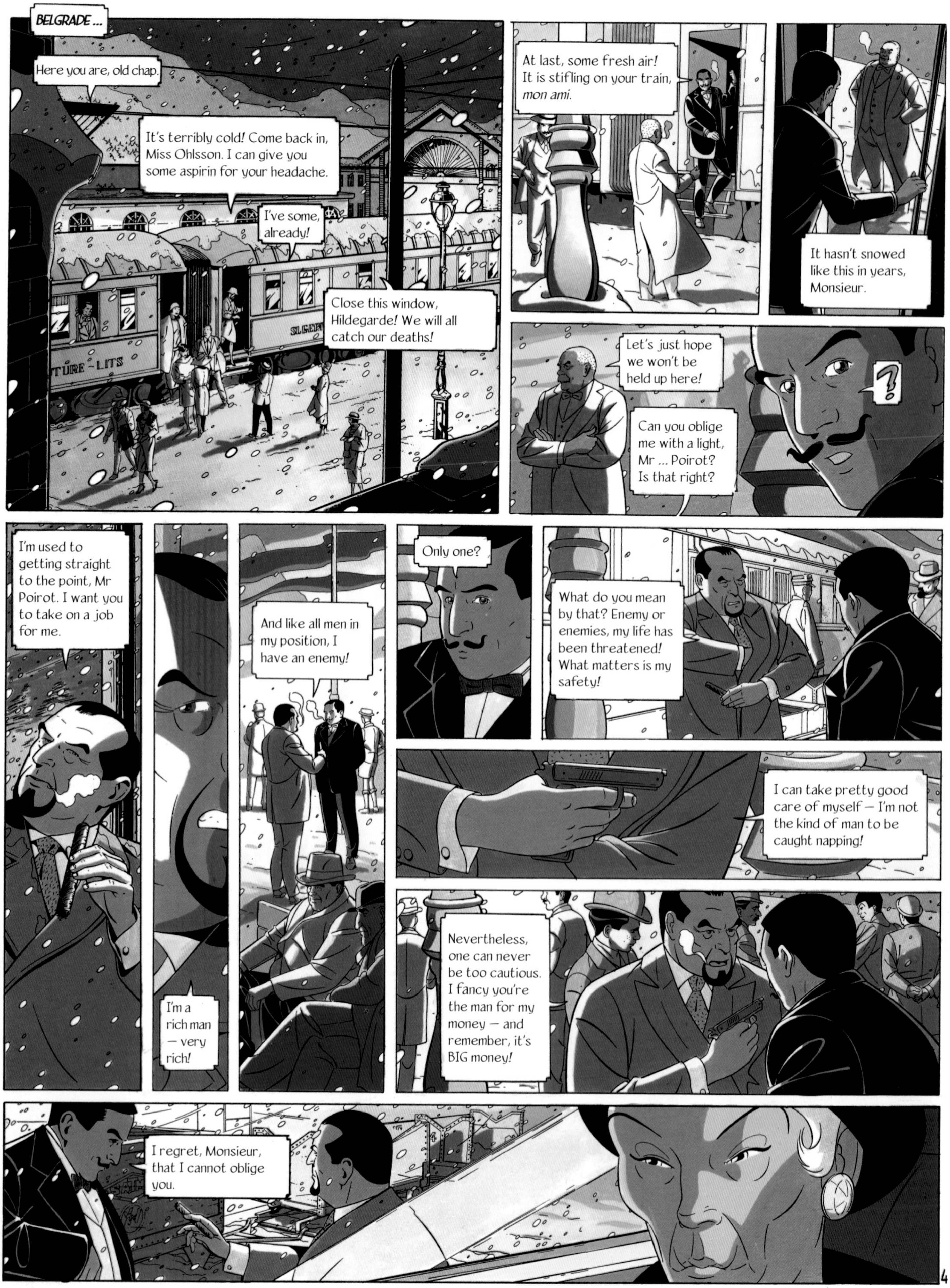

BELGRADE ...
Here you are, old chap.
It's terribly cold! Come back in, Miss Ohlsson. I can give you some aspirin for your headache.
I've some, already!
Close this window, Hildegarde! We will all catch our deaths!
At last, some fresh air! It is stifling on your train, *mon ami*.
It hasn't snowed like this in years, Monsieur.
Let's just hope we won't be held up here!
Can you oblige me with a light, Mr ... Poirot? Is that right?
?
I'm used to getting straight to the point, Mr Poirot. I want you to take on a job for me.
I'm a rich man — very rich!
And like all men in my position, I have an enemy!
Only one?
What do you mean by that? Enemy or enemies, my life has been threatened! What matters is my safety!
I can take pretty good care of myself — I'm not the kind of man to be caught napping!
Nevertheless, one can never be too cautious. I fancy you're the man for my money — and remember, it's BIG money!
I regret, Monsieur, that I cannot oblige you.

Name your price, Poirot!

You do not understand, Monsieur — *I refuse!*

I have been most fortunate in my profession. I take now only those cases ...

... which interest me!

Wait! Will twenty thousand dollars tempt you?

It will not.

If you're holding out for more, you won't get it! I know what a thing's worth!

I do too, Monsieur Ratchett!

Well then ... What's stopping you?

Au revoir!

Since you insist, Monsieur Ratchett — I do not like your face!

Why, I thought you'd left us. Weren't you getting off at Belgrade?

Just to stretch my legs a bit, Monsieur MacQueen. But I have been moved to my own compartment now ...

Oh, I see. So you are staying with us to Calais ...?

Good evening, sir.

Good evening, chère Madame.

You know, I'm dead scared of that man!

Oh, not the aide — his master. I've got a hunch about that man. His cabin is next to mine — with a communicating door!

Come, come, my dear lady! You have to calm down, if you want to enjoy a good night's sleep.

My daughter said I'd have an easy journey, but I don't feel happy!

You see, my daughter says I'm very intuitive, and I feel anything might happen tonight!

6

My daughter teaches at a big American college in Smyrna. Fortunately she is very sensible — you have to keep a cool head in these wild countries!

I'm sure she's right, *chère Madame.* Good night!

BOOM!

Funny! The train seems to have stopped!

CLiC

DRRR CLAC

Ratchett's cabin! What's that animal want now?

DRING

TOC TOC

RIL

TOC

IG

It's nothing. Sorry — my mistake!

DRING

Oh, *mon pauvre ami!* They're not going to let me sleep a wink on this train!

Twenty to one ...!

Mmmm ... ZZZZZZ!

Good grief! What a time to perform one's ablutions! This Ratchett is so inconsiderate!

I tell you, I didn't imagine it! A man was *hiding* in my compartment.

But it is impossible, Mrs Hubbard. The room is too small!

Oh well. Might as well join the fun, since everyone is up!

All this noise has made me thirsty!

You may go now.

Monsieur Pierre! A glass of water, *s'il vous plaît!*

I don't wish to appear tactless, but one can hear everything on this blessed train. What's up?

The American lady claims she woke up and saw a man in her compartment.

It's absurd! How could he have got out and left the door bolted on the inside? As if we didn't have enough worries already!

Worries ...?

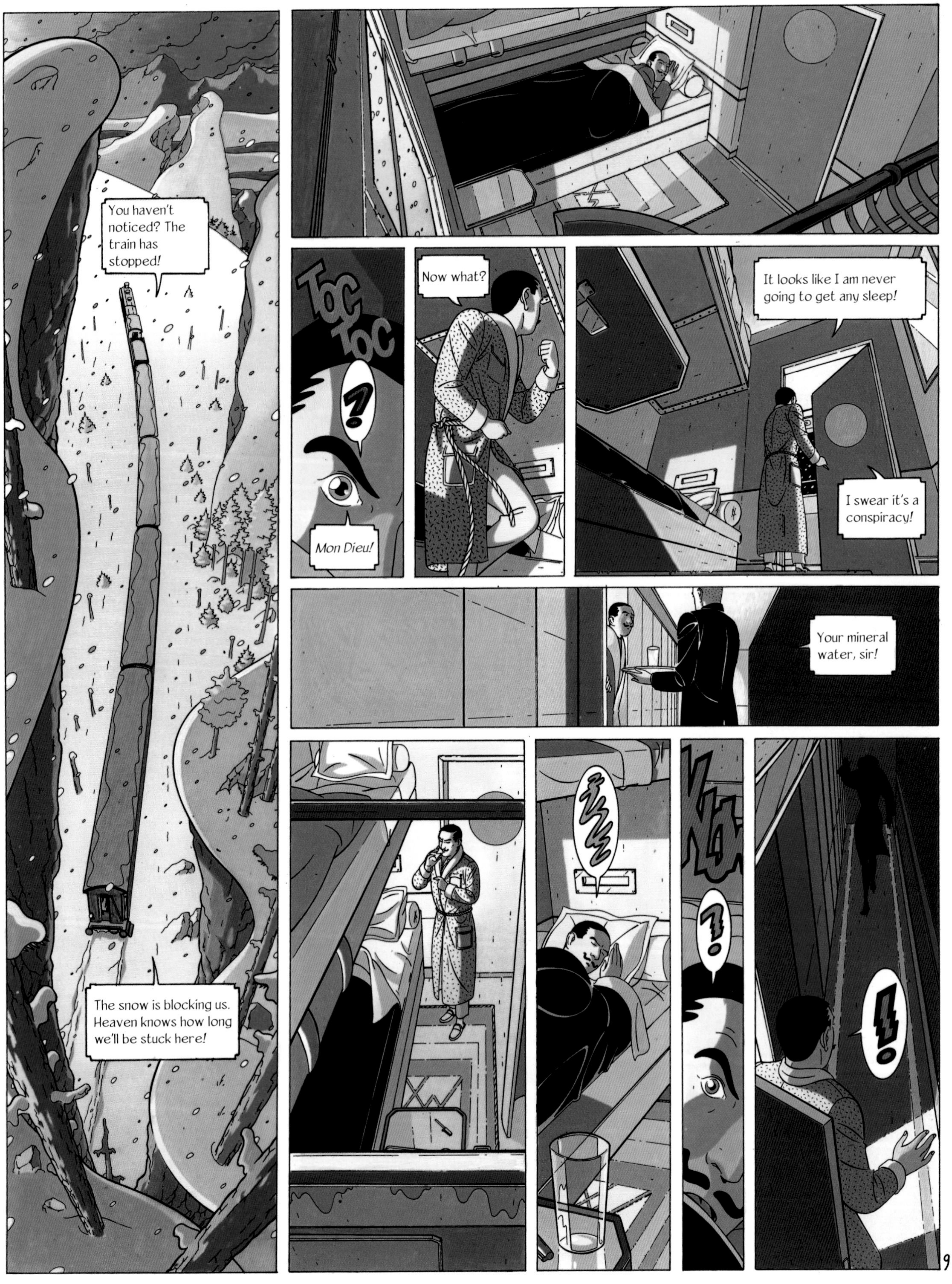
You haven't noticed? The train has stopped!
The snow is blocking us. Heaven knows how long we'll be stuck here!
TOC TOC
?!
Mon Dieu!
Now what?
It looks like I am never going to get any sleep!
I swear it's a conspiracy!
Your mineral water, sir!
?!
!!

This is a disaster! I have urgent business in Milan!

Too bad, old chap! But perhaps the driver will make up lost time.

Bravo, Miss Debenham. You're remarkably calm.

I try to avoid excitement, sir.

How philosophical! You're the strongest character here.

Oh, I know someone far far stronger than I am.

And that is ...?

Well, you may have noticed that ugly old lady.

Don't you think she controls herself exceptionally well, Monsieur, er ...?

Hercule Poirot! At your service, Madamoiselle.

Pardon, Monsieur. Could you join Monsieur Bouc? It's urgent!

It's terrible, Monsieur. A passenger was killed on the train last night!

What? Murdered? Who is stupid enough to get themselves killed on a luxury train?

Ratchett. The millionaire! *Killed on my train,* Poirot!

Mon ami, I beg you to take charge of the investigation before the Yugoslavian police starts poking its nose into the private lives of *my* passengers! Imagine the scandal!

I am touched by your faith. But it is a matter for the local police.

But we have been brought to a standstill in the middle of nowhere. We may be here for *days* before help can reach us!

Dr Constantine speaks words of wisdom!

Well, Poirot, will you accept?

Alright. But I must have complete freedom. And I need a plan of the sleeping coach with the names and passports of the passengers.

Agreed! We are all at your service.

Brr! Perishing! But at least we know how the culprit fled once the deed was done ...

No! The open window is just a ruse. The snow has ruined his plans.

No footprints! Nobody has left. The murderer is with us — ON THE TRAIN NOW!

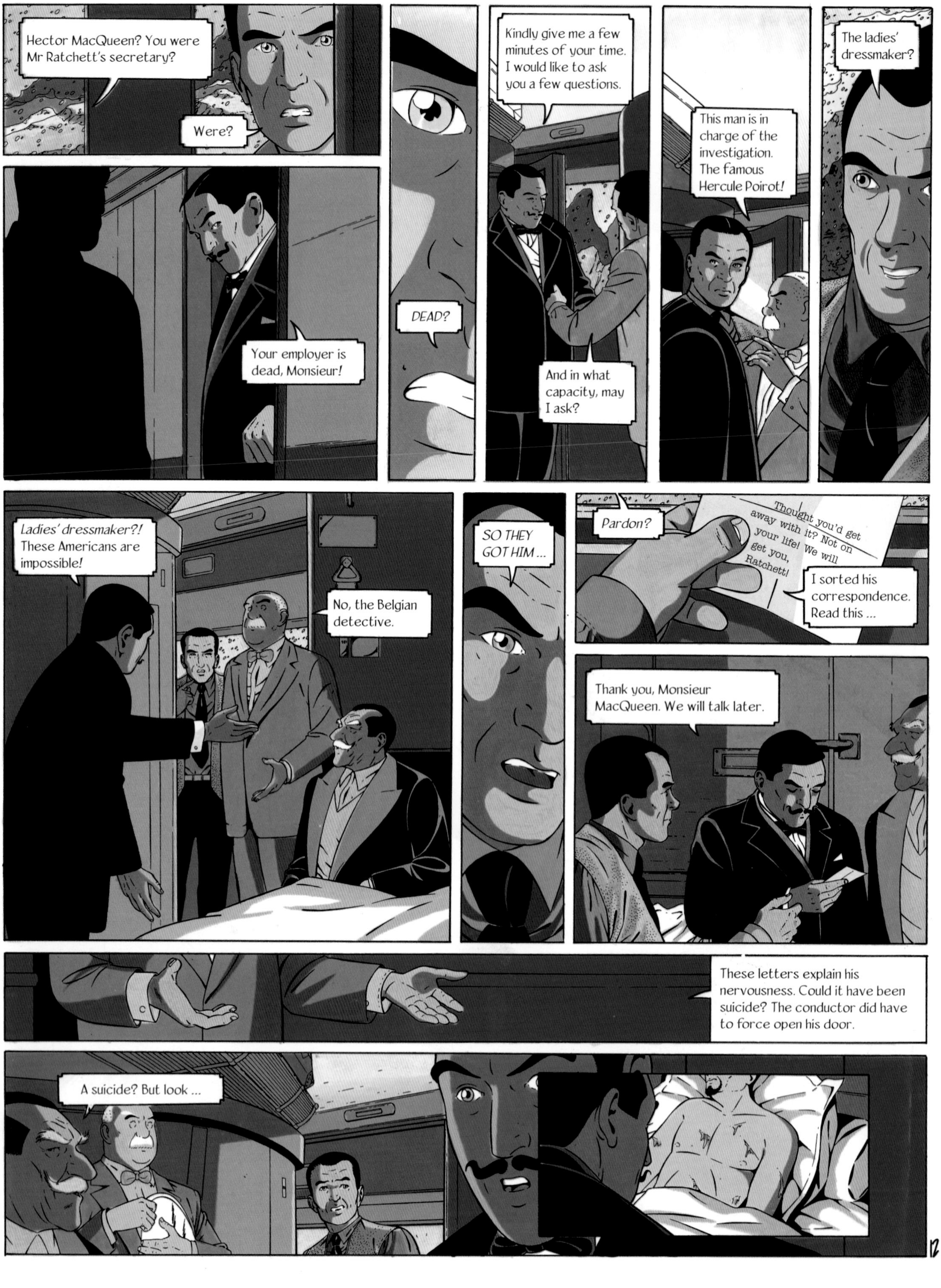

Hector MacQueen? You were Mr Ratchett's secretary?
Were?
Your employer is dead, Monsieur!
DEAD?
Kindly give me a few minutes of your time. I would like to ask you a few questions.
And in what capacity, may I ask?
This man is in charge of the investigation. The famous Hercule Poirot!
The ladies' dressmaker?
Ladies' dressmaker?! These Americans are impossible!
No, the Belgian detective.
SO THEY GOT HIM ...
Pardon?
Thought you'd get away with it? Not on your life! We will get you, Ratchett!
I sorted his correspondence. Read this ...
Thank you, Monsieur MacQueen. We will talk later.
These letters explain his nervousness. Could it have been suicide? The conductor did have to force open his door.
A suicide? But look ...
12

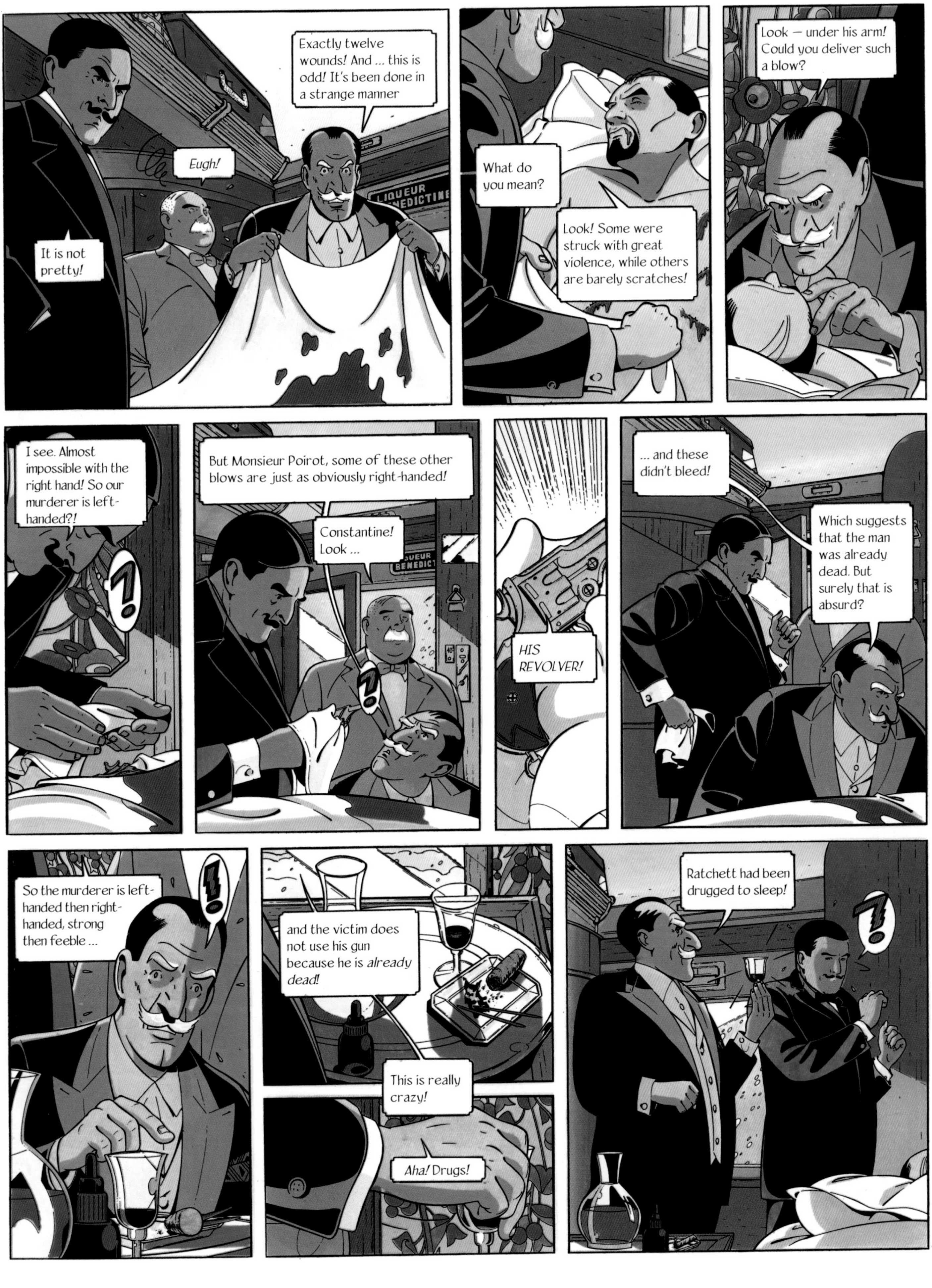
Exactly twelve wounds! And ... this is odd! It's been done in a strange manner
Eugh!
It is not pretty!
LIQUEUR BENEDICTINE
What do you mean?
Look! Some were struck with great violence, while others are barely scratches!
Look — under his arm! Could you deliver such a blow?
I see. Almost impossible with the right hand! So our murderer is left-handed?!
But Monsieur Poirot, some of these other blows are just as obviously right-handed!
Constantine! Look ...
HIS REVOLVER!
... and these didn't bleed!
Which suggests that the man was already dead. But surely that is absurd?
So the murderer is left-handed then right-handed, strong then feeble ...
and the victim does not use his gun because he is *already dead!*
This is really crazy!
Aha! Drugs!
Ratchett had been drugged to sleep!
13

Imagine — a second murderer who, coming in after the first, doesn't see in the darkness that he is merely stabbing a dead body ...

So there are *two* murderers on the train!

A man and a woman, perhaps?

Exactly! Some of these blows point to a certain weakness.

And who, if not a woman, could have dropped *THIS*?

How convenient! So the murderess leaves her handkerchief behind, marked with her initial. Just like in films!

Eh? I don't quite follow you, Poirot.

Don't try to follow me, *cher* Monsieur Bouc. For the moment I am just thinking out loud ...

Ah! And I overlooked this ...

Look, a pipe cleaner.

Not Ratchett's — we know he smoked cigars!

See here! We have the time of the crime!

I said the murder took place between midnight and two in the morning. And here is confirmation.

This compartment is full of clues, *Messieurs.* How can I be sure they have not been planted?

But I believe there is one clue that has not been faked — the burnt note left in this ashtray!

You know what I need ... an old-fashioned woman's hat-box!

Ah, Monsieur Pierre!

Would you be kind enough to do me a small favour?

Could you bring me the hat-boxes of two, *er*, slightly older ladies?

If they are not in their compartment, perhaps those of the Swedish lady and the Princess's maid?

Perfect! I just need to fetch something from my cabin ...

Are you going to tell us ...?

I will reheat the paper with these wire netting hat supports over the spirit stove I use for my moustaches ...

First one wire netting ...

The charred paper ...

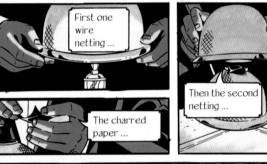

Then the second netting ...

Attention, Messieurs!

member little Daisy Armstrong

Voilà!

SSSCHRR

Gentlemen, I know the dead man's real name!

CASSETTI !!!

Ratchett — alias Cassetti. Doesn't this name ring a bell for you?

I recall — the kidnapping. A shocking affair!

This is the man who murdered Daisy Armstrong in America.

Colonel Armstrong was an English millionaire, awarded the Victoria Cross for bravery. He married the daughter of Linda Arden ...

... the most famous tragic American actress of her day. They had one child — little Daisy. She was three years old when she was kidnapped ...

Read all about it! Linda Arden's grand-daughter kidnapped! Gangsters demand enormous ransom!

The poor nursemaid, in a fit of despair, committed suicide. It was proved afterwards that she was absolutely innocent.

16

And the child?

Killed. Cassetti and his gang collected the ransom, even though she had been dead a fortnight.

What a horrible story!

That's not all: Mrs Armstrong was expecting another child. Devastated with grief, she gave birth to a dead baby and died in childbirth.

Her broken-hearted husband shot himself. A tragedy.

And that animal Cassetti escaped the electric chair?!

He was arrested. But thanks to his huge wealth and the secret hold he had on various people in authority, he was acquitted on some technicality.

The local people would definitely have lynched him, but he was clever enough to change his name and leave America.

Are there any members of the Armstrong family still alive?

I think I remember reading that Mrs Armstrong had a younger sister …

So we have the motive! But is it not an act of private vengeance or the work of some rival gang double-crossed by Cassetti?

I cannot regret that he is dead. But couldn't they have chosen some other place? Why my train?!

Indeed! Actually, your question is not quite as silly as it sounds.

OH!

17

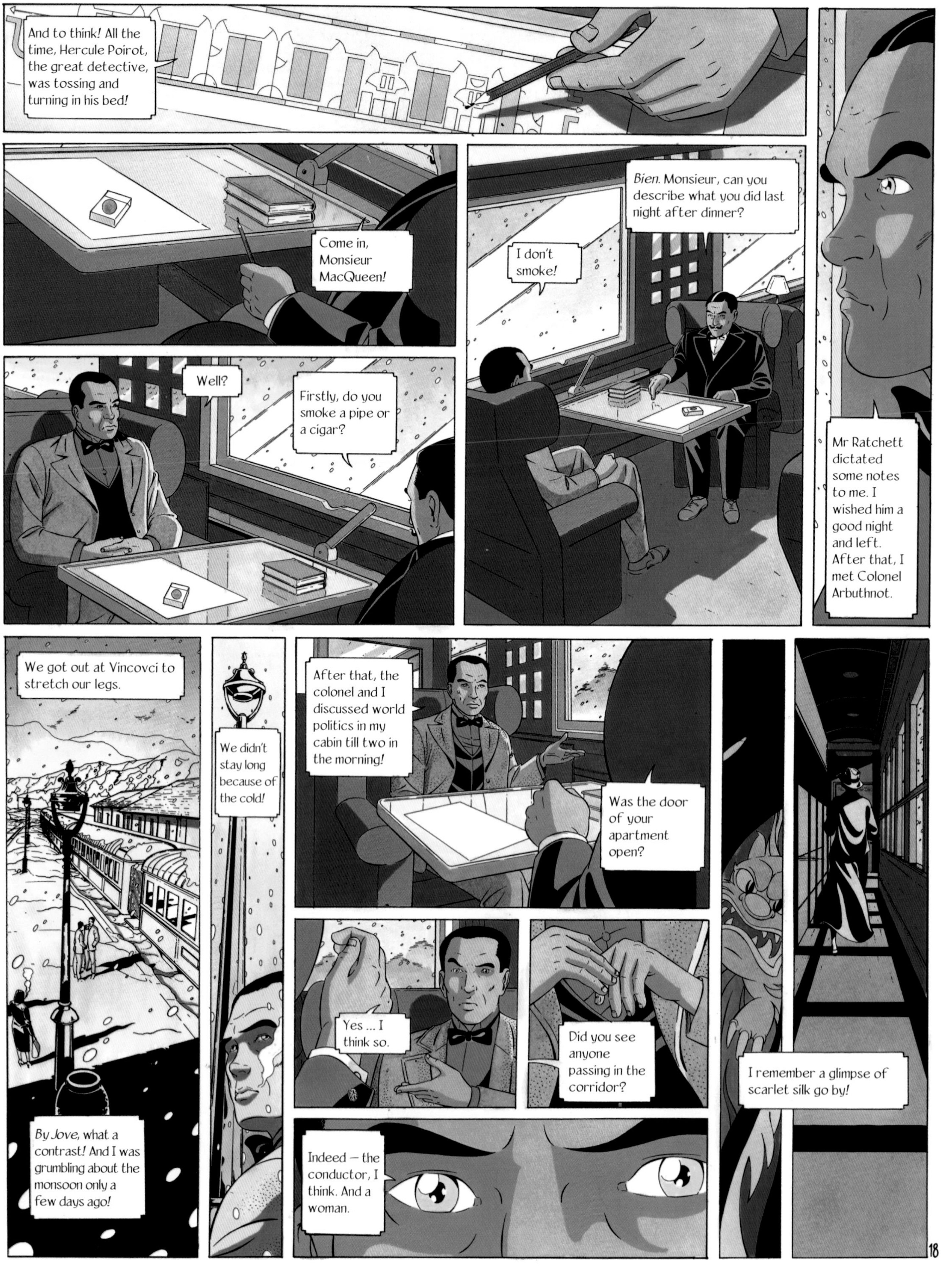

And to think! All the time, Hercule Poirot, the great detective, was tossing and turning in his bed!
Come in, Monsieur MacQueen!
Bien. Monsieur, can you describe what you did last night after dinner?
I don't smoke!
Well?
Firstly, do you smoke a pipe or a cigar?
Mr Ratchett dictated some notes to me. I wished him a good night and left. After that, I met Colonel Arbuthnot.
We got out at Vincovci to stretch our legs.
By Jove, what a contrast! And I was grumbling about the monsoon only a few days ago!
We didn't stay long because of the cold!
After that, the colonel and I discussed world politics in my cabin till two in the morning!
Was the door of your apartment open?
Yes ... I think so.
Did you see anyone passing in the corridor?
Indeed — the conductor, I think. And a woman.
I remember a glimpse of scarlet silk go by!
18

Did you suspect that Ratchett was a false name? That, in fact, he was Cassetti, the infamous kidnapper!

WHAT?

Oh! If I had known that, I would never have worked for the skunk! Never!

You feel strongly about the matter?

I have good reason to! My father was the District Attorney who handled the case. I remember Mrs Armstrong, a lovely woman — so gentle, so heartbroken. Cassetti deserved to die!

Good grief! It seems I'm incriminating myself!

Rest assured, I don't usually jump to hasty conclusions. Thank you, Monsieur MacQueen.

I've summoned Pierre Michel, but in my opinion, Monsieur Poirot, you already have your murderer. MacQueen looks like quite a hysterical person. I can just see him, in a fit of rage, stabbing his boss all over with a knife!

You think so, Monsieur Bouc?

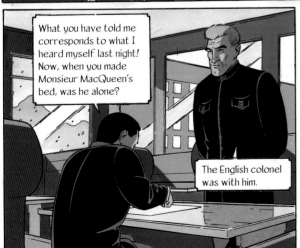

What you have told me corresponds to what I heard myself last night! Now, when you made Monsieur MacQueen's bed, was he alone?

The English colonel was with him.

One more thing! Who rang the bell when you were knocking on Monsieur Ratchett's door?

Ah!

The Russian lady. She asked me to send her maid!

La Princesse Dragomiroff...

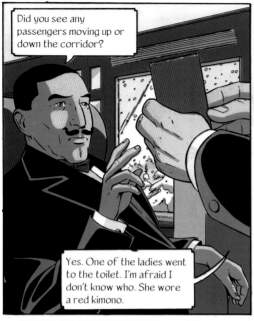

Did you see any passengers moving up or down the corridor?

Yes. One of the ladies went to the toilet. I'm afraid I don't know who. She wore a red kimono.

Do not distress yourself. You are not negligent. I see you are a widower?

Oh, for a long time now, Monsieur. My wife died of grief after the death of our twenty-year-old daughter.

May I go, sir?

Of course, Monsieur Pierre!

Ahem!

Edward Henry Masterman, I presume? You are Monsieur Ratchett's valet?

Was!

Yes, of course! Tell me, Masterman, did you notice anything strange in your master yesterday evening when he went to bed?

He was quite grumpy, but that wasn't unusual. He asked me angrily if I had left a letter on his bed. Of course, I hadn't!

Did he take sleeping drugs at all?

Always. He said he couldn't sleep on trains.

Indeed. After last night, I know the feeling!

Did he take one yesterday evening?

Yes, sir. I poured it into a glass ready for him.

Did Monsieur Foscarelli, who shares your compartment, go out at all last night?

I'm afraid not, sir!

I had a toothache and I just wanted to be quiet, but you know how talkative these Italians are ...

Ma que, it's your own fault! You eat too many English chocolates! I tell you, in Italy ...

So he speaks English?

Oh, it's more like pidgin English. But he told me that he had lived in America. In Chicago.

And neither one of you left the compartment during the night?

No, the Italian started snoring around ten thirty. As for me, I finally dropped off around four in the morning.

Tell me Masterman, have you heard of the Armstrong case?

!...

Of course I have. Hasn't everyone?

Thank you. By the way, do you smoke a pipe?

No, only cigarettes, sir.

It is urgent! I have some very important information. Who's in authority here?

I am, Madame Hubbard. What is it?

I called the conductor last night, sir, because a man was hiding in my cabin! And to think that it was the murderer! I'm still all of a flutter.

That stupid conductor didn't believe me. Well, now I've got proof of it!

I just found this on the magazine I was reading before going to sleep.

A button!

Check Pierre Michel's uniform!

And to top it all, the door connecting my cabin with the dead man's had not been bolted! The murderer obviously went through my room! Oh, wait till my daughter hears about this!

This door, Mrs Hubbard, why wasn't it locked beforehand?

Since I was already in bed, I asked the Swedish girl to check if it was properly locked.

Miss Ohlsson, a charming person! She had come to ask me for an aspirin. Just imagine, she opened Mr Ratchett's door by mistake. The poor thing was very distressed. She is not as brave as me! What's this?

Swedish girl?

I'm sorry, no. This handkerchief doesn't belong to me!

By the way, do you have a red silk dressing gown, Madame?

Certainly not!

My dressing gown is cosy pink flannel. And my handkerchiefs are sensible cotton things!

Finally — do you remember the kidnapping of the Armstrong baby?

Yes, indeed I do. The wretch who did it escaped, you know. You ask rather strange questions, Mr Poirot!

Are you quite sure he's a detective?

22

It's incomprehensible! Neither Pierre nor any other train employee is missing a button from their uniform ...

So we have the hypothesis of a false conductor. Perhaps a passenger in disguise?

You can make as many hypotheses as you wish, *mon ami!* Provided at least one is proved correct before the, *er* ... snowploughs arrive.

You mean "Hurry up before the police get involved." Say what you mean, Monsieur Bouc!

You knew it was me?

Someone who taps like a mouse on the door has to be the quietest person on the train.

Come in, Miss Ohlssen!

So, let us sum up what you have said: Madame Hubbard's door was locked. Furthermore, your room-mate, Miss Debenham, slept right through the night.

Yes, Monsieur. I'm a very light sleeper, and I would have heard her get up.

One last question: do you have a scarlet silk kimono?

No, I have a good comfortable dressing gown of pale mauve Jaeger material ... I hope you don't suspect me! As it is, I'm terribly shaken with all this!

What an emotional person! She was almost in tears when you raised the Armstrong case, even though she knew nothing about it.

Yes, very curious. And for an ex-nurse ... Come, Monsieur Bouc, let us go and pay a visit on Madame la Princesse Dragomiroff!

I always attend to the Princess. Whatever time it may be!

The time? I've no idea! I called Hildegarde last night for a massage. That's all. I belong to a generation which does not live with one eye on the clock, gentlemen!

Alright, Mademoiselle Hildegarde, perhaps you could be more precise if I ask you the colour of your dressing gown?

It is ...

Blue! Like mine. Why such questions? I have complete confidence in my maid.

You have been to America, I presume, Madame?

Yes, many times.

Were you acquainted with the Armstrongs, a family in which a tragedy occurred?

I must insist you answer me, Madame!

Sonia Armstrong, the child's mother, was my God-daughter! Whoever committed the crime deserved to be flogged to death!

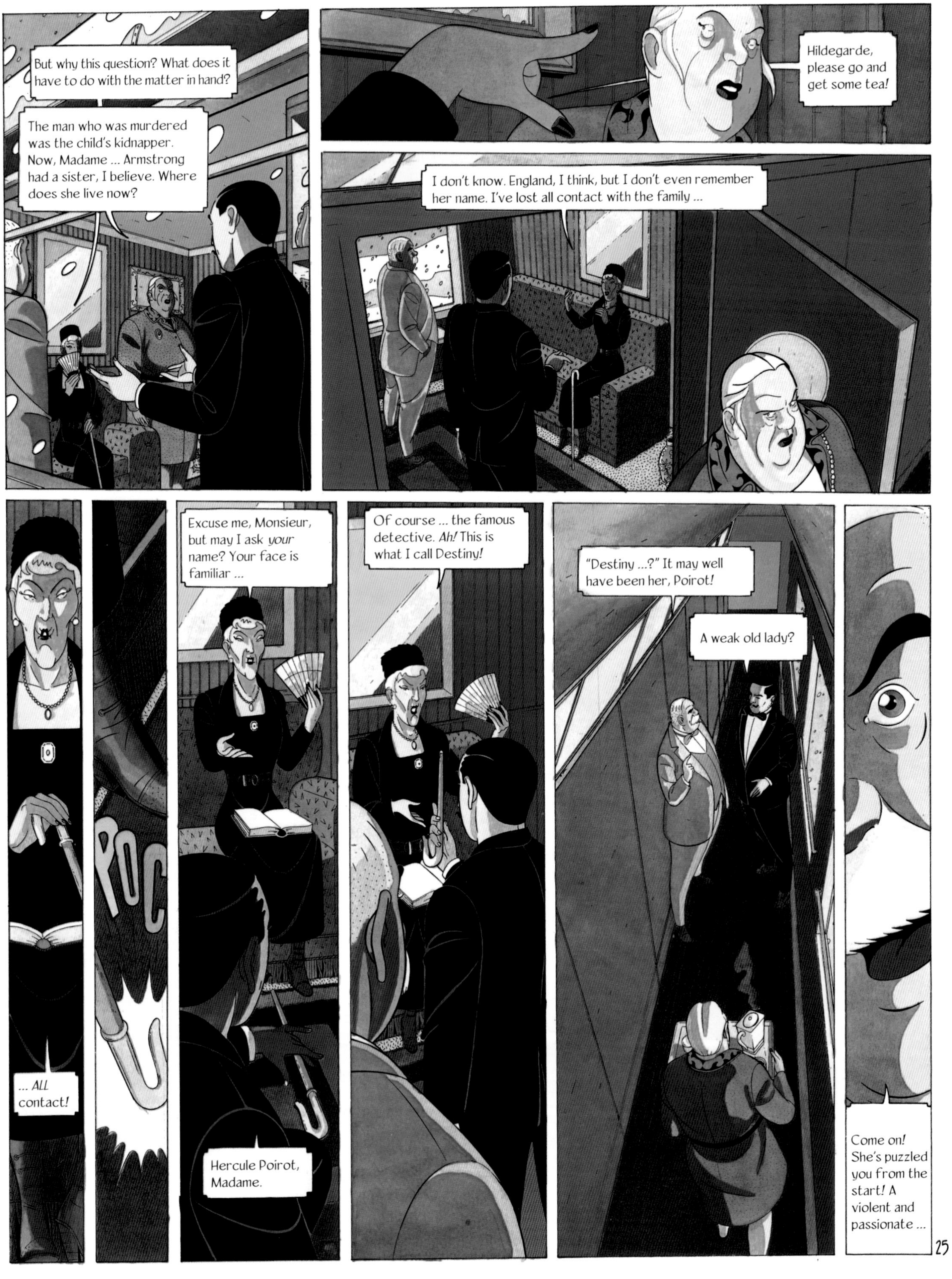
But why this question? What does it have to do with the matter in hand?
The man who was murdered was the child's kidnapper. Now, Madame ... Armstrong had a sister, I believe. Where does she live now?
Hildegarde, please go and get some tea!
I don't know. England, I think, but I don't even remember her name. I've lost all contact with the family ...
... ALL contact!
POC
Excuse me, Monsieur, but may I ask your name? Your face is familiar ...
Hercule Poirot, Madame.
Of course ... the famous detective. Ah! This is what I call Destiny!
"Destiny ...?" It may well have been her, Poirot!
A weak old lady?
Come on! She's puzzled you from the start! A violent and passionate ...
25

... oh! Sorry!

It is I who must apologize! Look — I have a handkerchief of yours, Mademoiselle Hildegarde ...

It's not mine!

The Princess's, perhaps?

No, "H" is not her initial. The Princess's name is *Natalia*.

One moment, Mademoiselle. When you went to the Princess last night, did you see anyone in the corridor?

Yes! A conductor pushed past me in a hurry. A small, dark man. He said *"pardon"* in a soft voice — like a woman's!

The description does not match Pierre Michel. So it must be a false conductor! But where did he go? We're getting nowhere!

Yes, we are, *mon cher*, slowly but surely ...

Hindered a little by a uniform and a dressing gown ... but these minor obstacles cannot stop Hercule Poirot!

Mon ami, you speak in riddles! Ah, Count Adrenyi!

What can I do for you? I understand you wish to question everyone.

Just a moment ...

Relax, my dear! I won't be long.

My wife is a fragile and delicate person, Gentlemen. I don't want her mixed up in this sordid business.

I fear I won't be able to do much to assist you. I slept through the night and didn't hear anything.

And the countess?

That is bad news. I mean for my investigation!

My wife always takes a sleeping draught on a train and retires early.

I see from your passport you were in America. Do you know the Armstrongs?

I was in Washington. America is a huge place — there must be hundreds of Armstrongs!

My dear, we weren't going to ...

Hush!

Thank you for coming, Madame.

May I ask you, did you accompany your husband on his trip to America?

No, Monsieur. We have only been married a year.

Ah, I see. It says on his passport "accompanied by his wife" — Elena Maria, maiden name Goldenberg, age 20.

It does now.

Careful, Poirot. It's a diplomatic passport. These people cannot possibly be involved.

But something is bothering me, mon vieux.

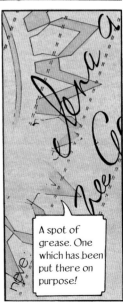

A spot of grease. One which has been put there on purpose!

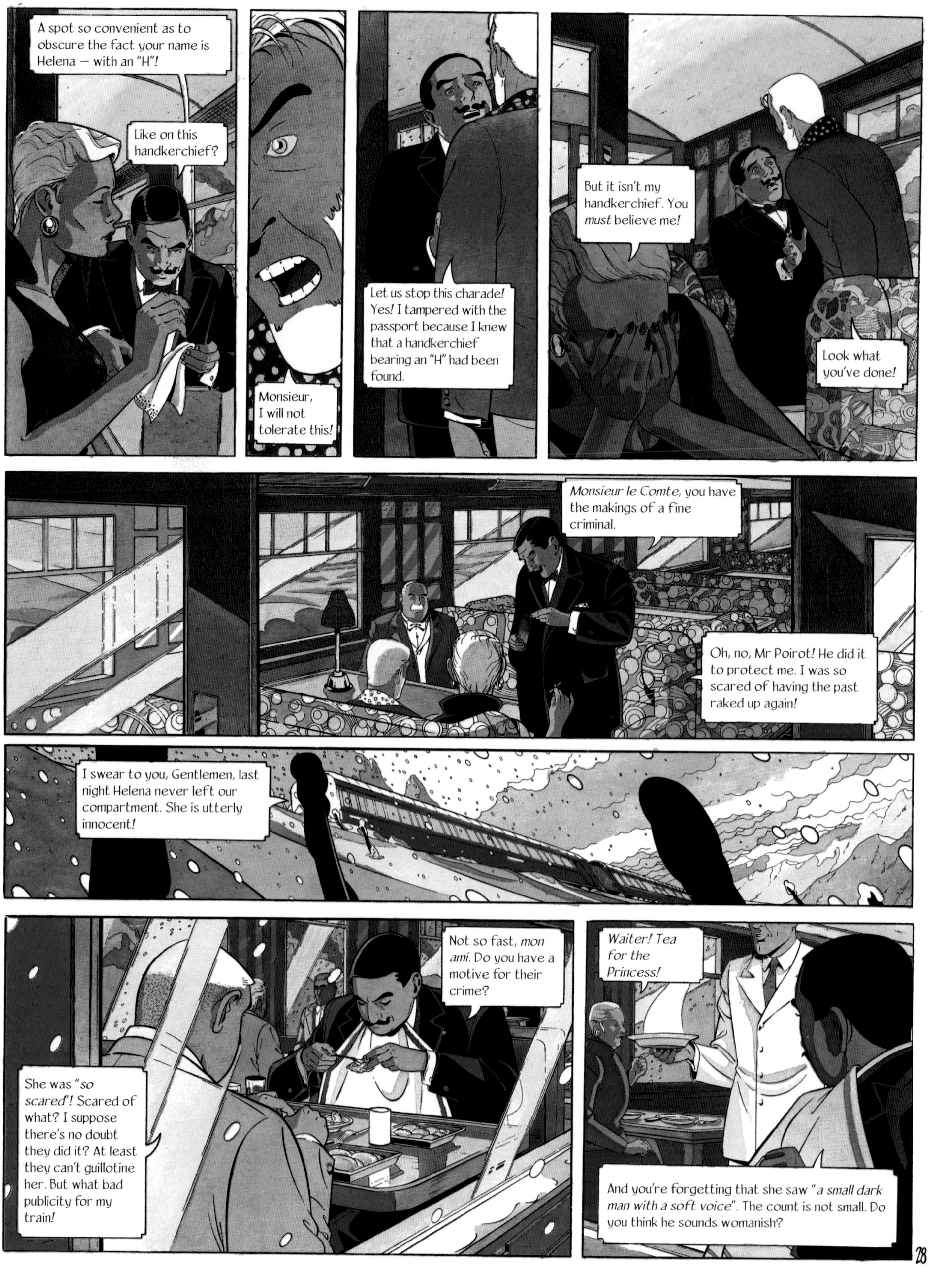
A spot so convenient as to obscure the fact your name is Helena — with an "H"!
Like on this handkerchief?
Monsieur, I will not tolerate this!
Let us stop this charade! Yes! I tampered with the passport because I knew that a handkerchief bearing an "H" had been found.
But it isn't my handkerchief. You *must* believe me!
Look what you've done!
Monsieur le Comte, you have the makings of a fine criminal.
Oh, no, Mr Poirot! He did it to protect me. I was so scared of having the past raked up again!
I swear to you, Gentlemen, last night Helena never left our compartment. She is utterly innocent!
Not so fast, *mon ami*. Do you have a motive for their crime?
She was "*so scared*"! Scared of what? I suppose there's no doubt they did it? At least they can't guillotine her. But what bad publicity for my train!
Waiter! Tea for the Princess!
And you're forgetting that she saw "*a small dark man with a soft voice*". The count is not small. Do you think he sounds womanish?
28

Foscarelli! This crime has all the hallmarks of a vendetta! The Italian has lived in Chicago, the capital of crime. Ratchett must've been killed by a Mafia rival!

Except that Foscarelli snored all through the night. That's what Masterman said.

Foiled again! What are you writing, *cher ami*?

The events in chronological order. It's strange how every alibi is confirmed by another witness.

AHHH! HELP! IT'S TOO HORRIBLE!

?

Madame Hubbard!

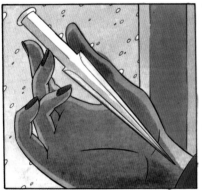

This horrible great knife — in my sponge-bag. *Covered in blood ...!*

!

MOMENTS LATER ...

It's horr...!

Here. Ooo ...

OH! MY HEAD!

But ...

Mmm!

Careful, Madame, it's cognac!

Yes, yes. I never touch spirits normally. My whole family are teetotallers.

Still, as this is medicinal ...

It's the weapon all right. It could have inflicted any one of the wounds on the body!

The weapon? But we know the blows were struck by two different people. Explain!

29

Some seem to have been struck by a man, some by a woman: a pipe-cleaner and a lace handkerchief ...

A red dressing gown, a uniform. All suggest a man and a woman!

"The small dark man with a womanish voice" could also be a woman in disguise ...

Always the dressing gown and the uniform! It's no good. Regardless of the company's reputation, I will have all luggage searched!

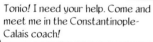

Tonio! I need your help. Come and meet me in the Constantinople-Calais coach!

If we follow this line of enquiry, the false conductor could have escaped into the corridor the moment Madame Hubbard was paralysed with fear and closed her eyes.

Pierre Michel came on the third ring, which was longer than the time needed to hide ...

But does the small man with the womanish voice *really exist*?

Signor Poirot? Antonio Foscarelli! I might as well answer your questions while my luggage is being ransacked!

Isn't this luxurious? I guess my business reputation would increase if I was travelled first class, *eh*?

I am an agent for Ford automobiles. America! Europe! I spend my life travelling!

I see. During the course of all your travels, did you hear about the Armstrong case?

Armstrong? No! But I meet so many clients! Let me give you some figures. Last year alone ...

Please, Monsieur. Let us not get sidetracked. Do you smoke a pipe?

Huh? No, cigarettes. *Ma que cosa?* Your questions are not very serious? You'll next want to know the colour of my socks! *Ha, ha, ha!*

I'm trying to get a criminal to confess, Monsieur.

You're speaking like the American police. Confess! That's all they know to say.

Indeed! you've had experience with the American police?

No! They could never get anything on me!

I'm an honest Italian citizen and I am expected in Milan on business. You can check for yourself. I've nothing to do with the crime!

Porca Madonna! First class upstarts!

Oaf!

Quite a show-off, eh? He's buttonholed me a few times. Thinks we're alike!

Ah, business rivalry! Monsieur Hardman, isn't it — the salesman? I've seen your passport.

A fake! Don't look surprised! Mr Ratchett had engaged my services. Here is my card ...

CYRUS HARDMAN
MCNEIL'S DETECTIVE AGENCY
NEW YORK

Yes, very reputable.

Ratchett was scared. Someone wanted to kill him. He had even given me the killer's description: a small man, dark, with a womanish kind of voice. Alas ...

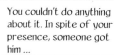

You couldn't do anything about it. In spite of your presence, someone got him ...

I certainly feel sore about it!

Didn't you realize who he was? Ratchett was Cassetti, the Armstrong murderer!

You don't say! I didn't recognize him! I was out West when it all happened.

Do you remember whether anyone involved in the case might have been a small dark man with a womanish voice?

There was a girl who threw herself out of the window ...

Can you give me a minute?

32

A LITTLE LATER ...

Yes, it was a veritable slaughter. Pretty much everyone to do with that case is dead.

Excuse me. The snow is blinding ...

IT'S NOT ME! I'M INNOCENT! I SWEAR IT!

Now what?

Poirot! We've found the uniform!

Ach! I didn't stuff it in there! I haven't opened my suitcase since Istanbul.

It's true!

We believe you. Seeing that he was blocked in by snow, the impostor had to get rid of the uniform somewhere.

Don't trust her, Poirot. *She* hid it!

I didn't do it!

I am sure you didn't. As sure as you are a good cook. You are a good cook, are you not?

Yes, indeed! All my employers have said so. I ...!

OH!

33

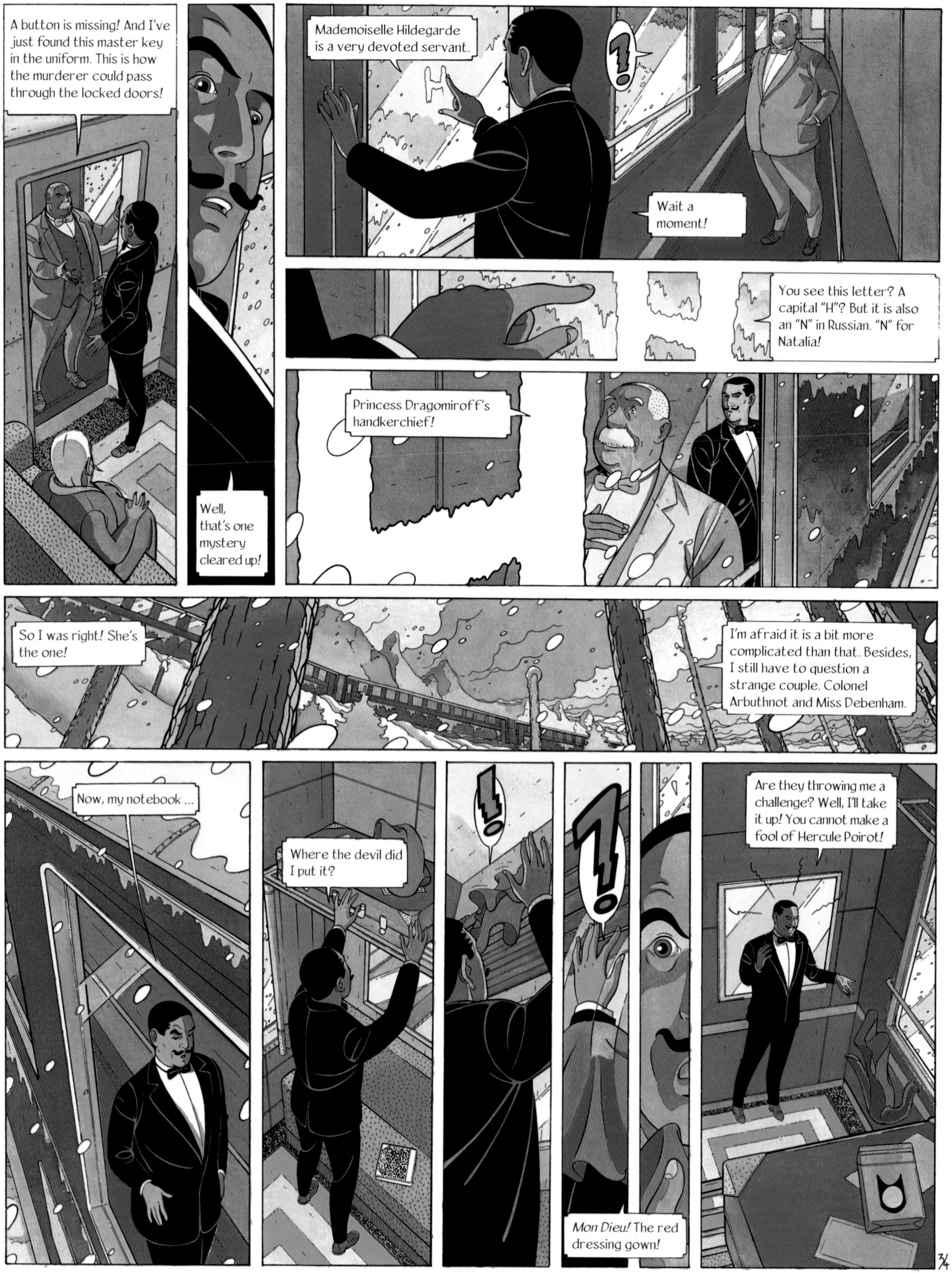
A button is missing! And I've just found this master key in the uniform. This is how the murderer could pass through the locked doors!
Well, that's one mystery cleared up!
Mademoiselle Hildegarde is a very devoted servant.
?!
Wait a moment!
You see this letter? A capital "H"? But it is also an "N" in Russian. "N" for Natalia!
Princess Dragomiroff's handkerchief!
So I was right! She's the one!
I'm afraid it is a bit more complicated than that. Besides, I still have to question a strange couple. Colonel Arbuthnot and Miss Debenham.
Now, my notebook ...
Where the devil did I put it?
!
?!
Mon Dieu! The red dressing gown!
Are they throwing me a challenge? Well, I'll take it up! You cannot make a fool of Hercule Poirot!
34

Countess!

Yes! You Madame! Am I not speaking to Linda Arden's daughter?

How ...?

How did I guess? The *little grey cells*, Madame!

You were scared of so many ghosts from the past. And then a lie from the Princess: she claims that she doesn't remember your name. Why would she say that?

Because she recognized you on the train!

I didn't go into this Ratchett's cabin. I swear it!

Let's leave that aside. I need to "rake up the past", Madame. You were a child when this tragedy happened. What was the name of your governess?

I don't recall, it was so long ago. Er ... Miss Freebody, that's it! But why do you want to know?

So I can discover the truth!

THE WHOLE TRUTH!

Colonel Arbuthnot, you're the only one who smokes a pipe on this train.

Well, is it a crime?

We found a pipe-cleaner near the dead man. Is it yours?

I don't write my regimental number in it!

Monsieur, if this conversation is going to take an accusatory turn, I don't want it to take place in front of someone who is a stranger to me!

Really?

That's what you'd have me believe! Yesterday I spotted you in Istanbul, and later I overheard a conversation between the two of you ...

Colonel Arbuthnot, what did you mean by: "Mary, I want to see you out of all this"?

I can't answer you. I have my loyalty.

And you, Mademoiselle, what did your reply mean: "When it's all over"?

It was a private conversation. You're asking an indiscreet question, and I will not reply!

Passion? I only see cold Anglo-Saxon lack of emotion!

Cast your mind back ...

I had the opportunity to watch you before we boarded the train. I also have reason to believe that the dead man was known to you.

In fact, Mr Poirot, since the victim was knifed to death, it looks to me like a crime of passion. Believe me, I can think of better things to do than murdering a stranger ...

Stop your imaginings. This incident does not concern me in any way.

And you don't know anything about the Armstrong case?

No, I do not.

And you, Colonel?

I read about it in the papers. I knew of Toby Armstrong, that's all. Nice fellow. Received the Victoria Cross.

Ratchett was the one who killed little Daisy Armstrong.

In that case, the swine deserved what he got!

Don't get me wrong. As an officer I would have preferred to see him tried by a jury and hanged. I prefer law and order to private vengeance.

Miss Debenham, you are lying! You knew the Armstrongs personally! Countess Adrenyi practically told me that you were her governess in New York.

She did?

Yes. Unwittingly, mind you! The countess lies very badly, which is all to her credit, and told me that her governess was called Miss Freebody.

Freebody. Like the "Debenham & Freebody" shop in London. An unfortunate association of ideas, is it not?

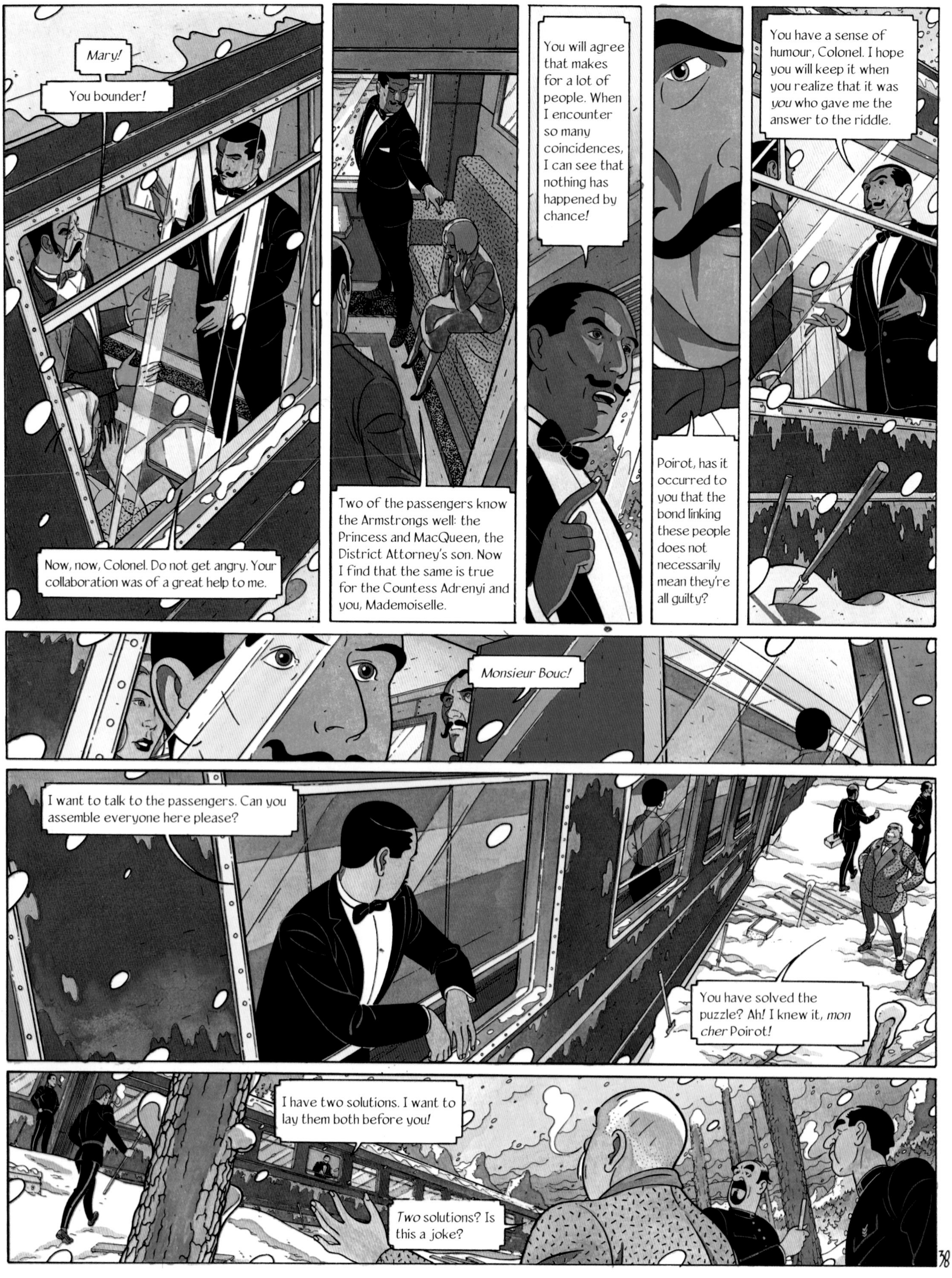
Mary!
You bounder!
Now, now, Colonel. Do not get angry. Your collaboration was of a great help to me.
Two of the passengers know the Armstrongs well: the Princess and MacQueen, the District Attorney's son. Now I find that the same is true for the Countess Adrenyi and you, Mademoiselle.
You will agree that makes for a lot of people. When I encounter so many coincidences, I can see that nothing has happened by chance!
Poirot, has it occurred to you that the bond linking these people does not necessarily mean they're all guilty?
You have a sense of humour, Colonel. I hope you will keep it when you realize that it was *you* who gave me the answer to the riddle.
Monsieur Bouc!
I want to talk to the passengers. Can you assemble everyone here please?
You have solved the puzzle? Ah! I knew it, *mon cher* Poirot!
I have two solutions. I want to lay them both before you!
Two solutions? Is this a joke?
38

Messieurs et Mesdames, my investigations have led me to the following conclusions!

THE MURDERER IS ONE OF US!

GOOD LORD!

At least, that *was* my theory!

What do you mean?

I have a simple theory. The murderer, disguised as a conductor, entered the train at Vincovci to kill Ratchett. He got rid of the weapon, then the uniform, and disappeared just the same way he came.

Monsieur Poirot! You're forgetting the time of the crime shown by Mr Ratchett's watch: a quarter-past one. The train was already blocked by snow!

Pah!

Ratchett omitted to put his watch back an hour, which was still on Eastern European time. It was a quarter-past twelve!

An absurd explanation!

Your conclusion is over-simplistic and has many loose ends. It does not hold water.

My second theory is very different, but you may not like it!

Let us leave aside the details: the pipe-cleaner, the handkerchief, the uniform, the dark man and that blessed red dressing gown ... all put there to put me off the scent!

Let us consider what all of you have told me ...

Correct! It is just a hypothesis. But do not abandon it too abruptly. You may agree with it later.

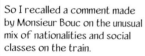

I find that four of you know the Armstrong family. Four out of twelve! But why would I stop there?

So I recalled a comment made by Monsieur Bouc on the unusual mix of nationalities and social classes on the train.

It reminded me of rich American households where you might find an English governess, a Swedish nurse, an Italian chauffeur, a French maid ...

Such imagination!

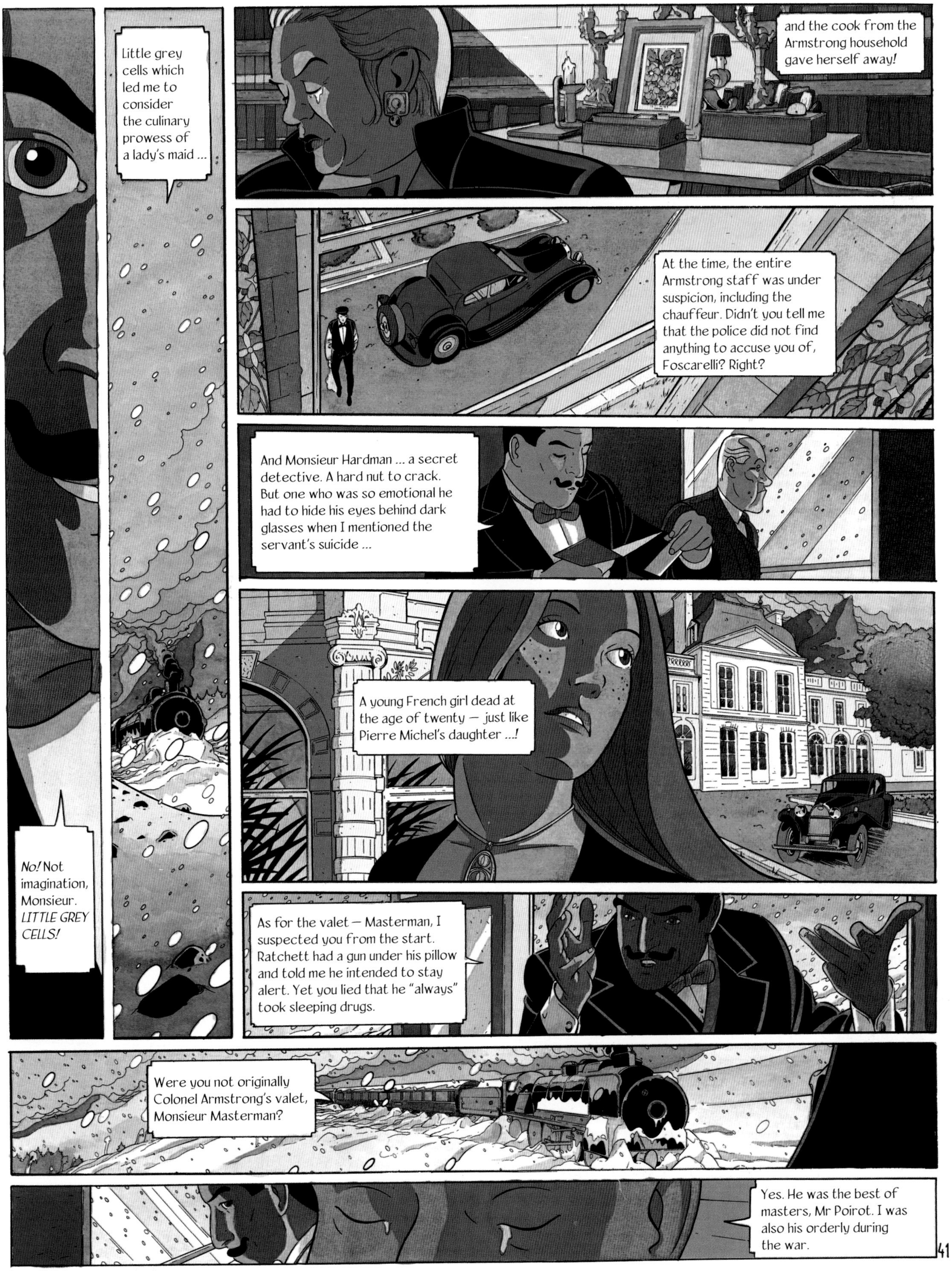

Little grey cells which led me to consider the culinary prowess of a lady's maid ...
and the cook from the Armstrong household gave herself away!
At the time, the entire Armstrong staff was under suspicion, including the chauffeur. Didn't you tell me that the police did not find anything to accuse you of, Foscarelli? Right?
And Monsieur Hardman ... a secret detective. A hard nut to crack. But one who was so emotional he had to hide his eyes behind dark glasses when I mentioned the servant's suicide ...
A young French girl dead at the age of twenty — just like Pierre Michel's daughter ...!
No! Not imagination, Monsieur. LITTLE GREY CELLS!
As for the valet — Masterman, I suspected you from the start. Ratchett had a gun under his pillow and told me he intended to stay alert. Yet you lied that he "always" took sleeping drugs.
Were you not originally Colonel Armstrong's valet, Monsieur Masterman?
Yes. He was the best of masters, Mr Poirot. I was also his orderly during the war.
41

Thus they are all accomplices. But who is the culprit?

Surely you don't expect *us* to tell you?

You're mistaken, Colonel. *You* gave me the solution! Your remark about a jury!

A court jury has *twelve* members. *Twelve* suspects! *Twelve* wounds on the body!

Your reasoning is flawed — because you are also incriminating the conductor!

Tut tut! Think about what we know. Countess Adrenyi is a fragile person ...

So her husband saved her from this painful task.

For Helena, who is still suffering!

For my little Daisy ...

whom I loved so much!

42

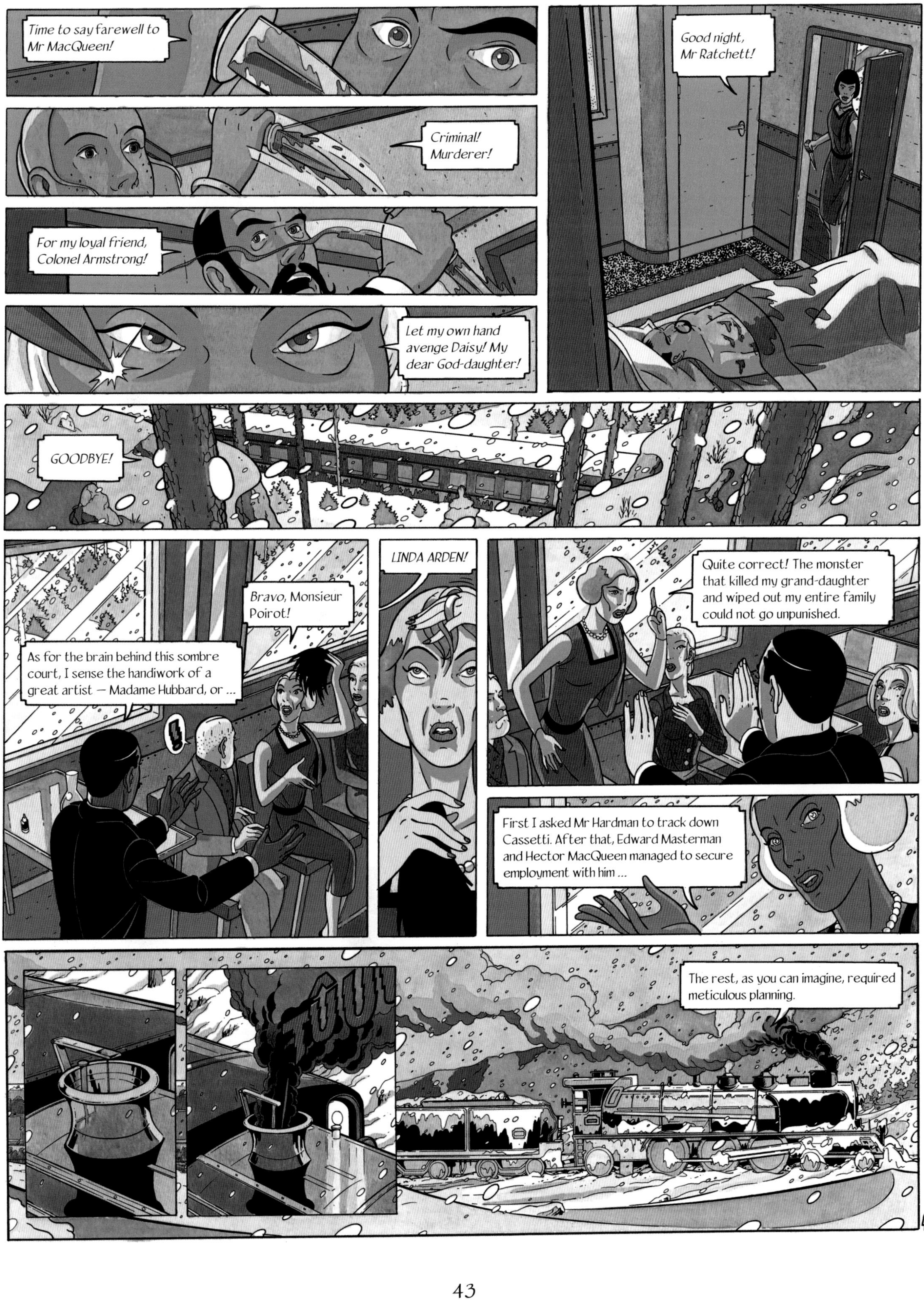
Time to say farewell to Mr MacQueen!
Criminal! Murderer!
For my loyal friend, Colonel Armstrong!
Let my own hand avenge Daisy! My dear God-daughter!
Good night, Mr Ratchett!
GOODBYE!
Bravo, Monsieur Poirot!
As for the brain behind this sombre court, I sense the handiwork of a great artist — Madame Hubbard, or ...
!
LINDA ARDEN!
Quite correct! The monster that killed my grand-daughter and wiped out my entire family could not go unpunished.
First I asked Mr Hardman to track down Cassetti. After that, Edward Masterman and Hector MacQueen managed to secure employment with him ...
TUUT
The rest, as you can imagine, required meticulous planning.
43

The police would have concluded that a murderer came from outside, as in the first hypothesis, but the snow disrupted your plans.

AND THEN I TURNED UP! So you had to put obstacles in my path!

I must say, the red dressing gown charade was not bad at all!

Monsieur! The Armstrong tragedy has marked us all for life!

Indeed!

Did I not tell you, Monsieur Bouc, that you could *choose* from two solutions?

Hmm ... I think your first theory should satisfy the police, Monsieur Poirot.

Doctor Constantine?

Well, as far as the forensic evidence is concerned, I think, er, I might have made a few mistakes!

Then, *Mesdames et Messieurs*, I retire from the case.

Time to have another glass of your delicious *vin rouge*, Monsieur Bouc ...

AGATHA CHRISTIE (1890–1976) is known throughout the world as *The Queen of Crime.* Her first book, *The Mysterious Affair at Styles,* was written during the First World War and introduced us to Hercule Poirot, the Belgian detective with the "Little Grey Cells", who was destined to reappear in nearly 100 different adventures over the next 50 years. Agatha also created the elderly crime-solver, Miss Marple, as well as more than 2,000 colourful characters across her 80 crime novels and short story collections. Agatha Christie's books have sold over one billion copies in the English language and another billion in more than 100 countries, making her the best-selling novelist in history. Now, following years of successful adaptations including stage, films, television, radio, audiobooks and computer games, some of her most famous novels, starting with *Murder on the Orient Express, Death on the Nile* and *The Murder of Roger Ackroyd,* have been adapted into comic strips so that they may be enjoyed by yet another generation of readers.

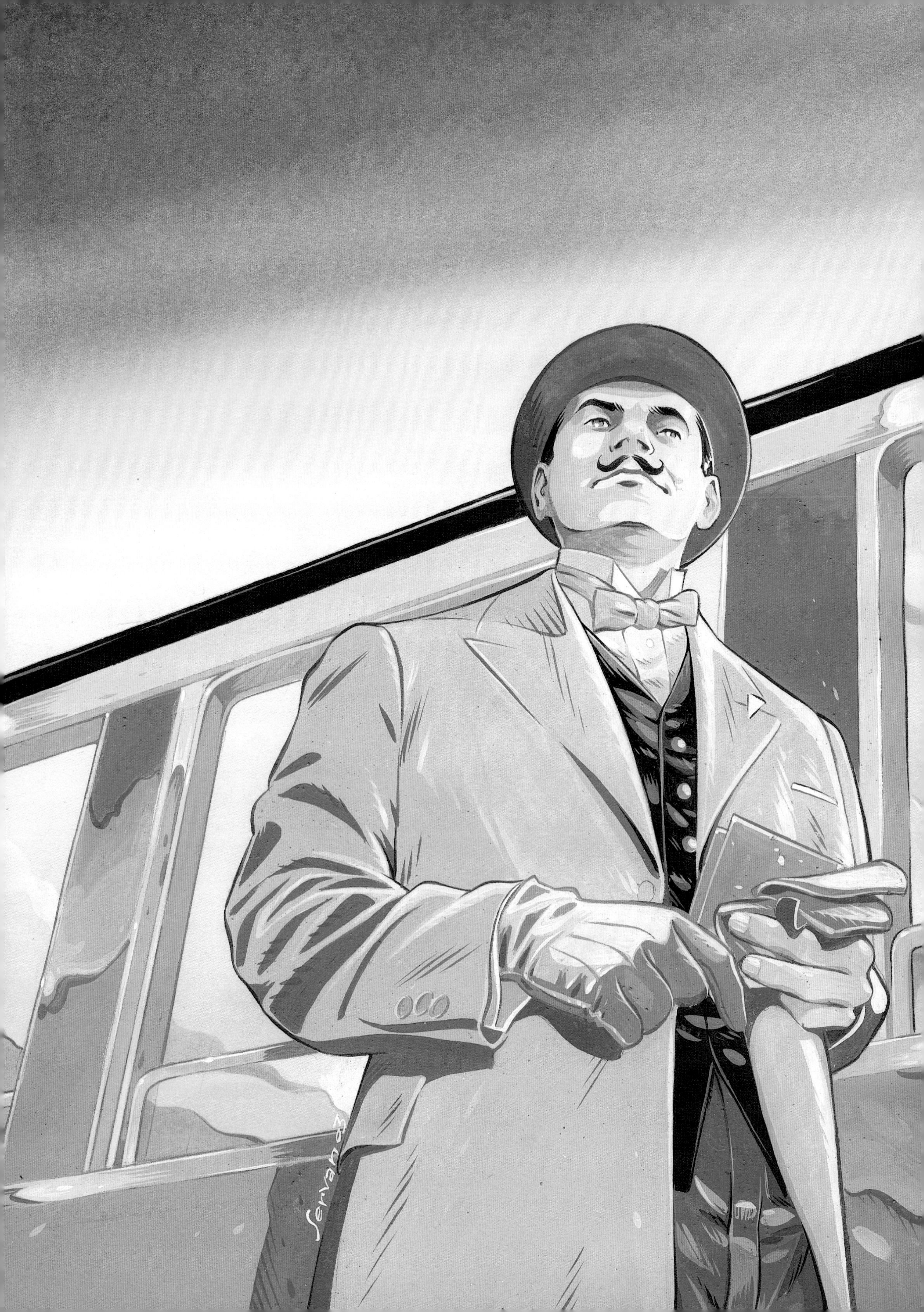